P9-CLD-169

STRATFORD

STRATFORD

Photography by Richard Bain

Foreword by Christopher Plummer

The BOSTON
MILLS PRESS

Copyright © 1998 Richard Bain and Christopher Plummer

Published in 1998 by
Boston Mills Press
132 Main Street
Erin, Ontario
N0B 1T0
Tel 519-833-2407
Fax 519-833-2195
www.boston-mills.on.ca

Distributed in Canada by
General Distribution Services Inc.
30 Lesmill Road
Toronto, Canada M3B 2T6
Tel 416-445-3333
Fax 416-445-5967
e-mail gdsinc@genpub.com
TELEBOOK S1150391

Distributed in the United States by
General Distribution Services Inc.
85 River Rock Drive, Suite 202
Buffalo, New York 14207-2170
Toll-free 1-800-805-1083
Fax 1-800-481-6207
e-mail gdsinc@genpub.com
PUBNET 6307949

02 01 00 99 98   1 2 3 4 5

CATALOGUING IN PUBLICATION DATA

Bain, Richard (Richard G.), 1954–
Stratford

ISBN 1-55046-274-1

1. Stratford (ont.) — Pictorial works. I. Title.

Fc3099.S77B34 1998   971.3'23   C98-930339-X
F1059.5.S72B34 1998

Design by Gillian Stead
Printed in Canada

BOSTON MILLS BOOKS are available for bulk purchase for sales promotions, premiums,
fundraising, and seminars. For details contact:

SPECIAL SALES DEPARTMENT, Stoddart Publishing Co. Limited, 34 Lesmill Road,
Toronto, Ontario, Canada M3B 2T6   Tel 416-445-3333 Fax 416-445-5967

For my parents

The Stratford Festival Theatre, surrounded by parkland and located along the Avon River, is the largest classical repertory theatre in North America.

The rolling countryside near Sebringville.

A favourite hero of mine, Stephen Leacock, once confessed that for the small Ontario town he had the greatest affection. "The great fascination of the small Ontario town," he wrote, "is that it seemed to grow from infancy to old age within a human lifetime." He fictionalized his by calling it Mariposa. We all have our Mariposas. Mine happens to be Stratford.

In Stratford I have lived, laughed, loved, laboured and learned. That was long ago — almost forty years. Still, whenever I take a right off the flat, charmless 401 onto the far more inviting trail that winds through the beginnings of rolling farm country, where the shadows chase themselves across the fields, I can't help smiling as a rush of memories escort me back to the vivid scenes of my professional youth and the town that became such a part of me.

Stratford — before the Festival exploded upon it like so many fireworks — had enjoyed a substantially long and successful innings as a modestly well-heeled, respectable Presbyterian–Anglican community largely dependent on agriculture and the manufacture of furniture. It stood in the County of Perth, with the Irish to the north and the Germans to the east. It boasted no particular architectural style; in appearance it was both functional and picturesque. The picturesque part was the river. In 1832 or thereabouts, they called the river the Little Thames. Encouraged on its way by a purposeful, steady current, it snaked through town and out into the country, narrowing as it went, and finally ended a few miles south, where it joined, you guessed it, the Big Thames.

Round about 1856, when the Grand Trunk Railway imposed itself on "Stratters" and became a major employer, some observant soul must have twigged that the river had been wrongly christened. The correction was made and it became the Avon, after its famous older brother in Blighty. As a haven-on-the-Avon, our Stratford continued into the first half of the twentieth century in contentment and peace. Its recreations were curling and skating in winter, bowling and boating in summer. The sound of bagpipes was often heard in the land, and the good citizens looked for any excuse they could find to get into their kilts. Most entertainment centred around the river. The swans, the river's rightful guardians, glided about year after year, looking for all the world as if they were auditioning for *Lohengrin*. Life was altogether unhurried. Like the river, it had found its rhythm.

Tom Patterson,
a man with a dream,
stands on the island
named in his honour.

Then one day Tom Patterson, a wily local journalist in love with bowties, came home from the Wars and decided it was high time his town produced something to justify its name. Now Tom has a feisty charm, a caustic wit and oodles of imagination, so it didn't take him long to persuade a few important townfolk to help promote his dream. Eventually they raised enough money to telegraph Tyrone Guthrie in Ireland. A towering giant with a formidable beak-nose, Dr. Guthrie just happened to be one of the theatre world's most Olympian of gods. The telegram politely suggested he take a leap of some 2,000 miles, come straight over and start a festival. Well, Tom and his friends couldn't believe their luck, for the good doctor recognized at once that a wonderfully reckless madness had clearly taken hold of them and, being quite wonderfully mad himself, without a moment's hesitation, he accepted.

The Great Northern Eagle had landed. On his arm, almost as tall, was Tanya Moisievitch, a stately lady of serene beauty and one of the world's most brilliant creators of sets and costumes. They fell for Stratford. They fell for Tom's dream. They fell for Tom. They even fell for Tom's little band, who would call themselves the Board — the best board anyone could ever want; perhaps not equipped with infinite resources or the most powerful connections, but blessed with the kind of faith, intelligence and passion that money just can't buy. There they stood, their uplifted faces telling the whole story, eager to begin, ready to go to any lengths for this new Messiah — waiting, waiting for the Word.

The Festival Theatre silhouetted against a late-summer sun.

The Word came.

Money — raise it. That hill by the river? That'll be it! Dig a hole — build an amphitheater — Tanya will design it — we'll put a tent over it — cheaper that way — we'll get that chap from Chicago — Skip Manley — best tent-man there is. Remember, disaster may strike — rise above! And not to worry — you've already got swans. I'll choose the plays and the actors. You'll need a star — I'll bring one. Don't forget costumes — Tanya will design them. V. essential — give jobs to the locals, they'll love it — and whatever you do, get the town behind you — make 'em feel it's theirs — it'll belong to them, you know. Good luck.

The race was on. Somehow money was found. Shapes began to emerge. April winds whistled under the tarpaulins. Actors with blue, chapped lips trying to mouth iambic pentameter. Tanya's platform already assuming a timeless dignity. There was a long way to go, but excitement was high when suddenly — disaster. Everything stopped. All building ceased. No more money. The race was over.

But something remarkable occurred. Whether brought forth by Tanya's unfinished Doric columns, bathed in moonlight and evoking ancient Greece and the promise of glory, one will never know, but the spirit of Marathon had undoubtedly descended upon the town, for the head contractor, Oliver Gaffney, in an extraordinary gesture of sacrifice and goodwill, offered to waive his fee, and one by one the workers returned, vowing to finish the job without pay. High on a rigging, Skip Manley, wearing his crown of olives proudly, if slightly askew, called down, "We'll finish your tent for ya. Pay us when y'can!"

The race resumed, torches were passed, the finishing line was in sight. On the eve of July 13, 1953, welcomed by a flurry of trumpets, a large international crowd gathered somewhat apprehensively outside the Tent. Major press from England, the U.S. and Canada stood about in little groups, wondering why they had come so far. But once inside, they sat humbled and spellbound by the purity of Tanya's noble structure, waiting on the edge of their seats for the Games to begin. Somewhere up on a hill a cannon boomed. A silence fell over the multitude — the low, sonorous sound of a gong gave the signal — the runners came out into the light — the miracle was upon us and Tom Patterson's dream was up and away!

The fanfare announces the start of each performance at the Festival Theatre.

Overleaf: *The Perth County Court House and the distinctive double arches of the Huron Street bridge.*

The bust of William Shakespeare in the Shakespearean Gardens.

1956 — I arrive for my first season. Am driving up the 401 with Herbie Whittaker, Canada's top critic. It's the last year of the Tent, so everyone's still feeling pioneerish. In my mid-twenties, I'm to play the plum part of Henry V — *quel coup*! I've just been in a big Broadway success, so I swan in, arrogant as hell and quite insufferable. We are quaffing ale at the old Windsor Hotel on Albert Street, in one of those sinister, ill-smelling dens called Beverage Rooms (men only), a now long-extinct reminder of colonial puritanism and antiquated liquor laws. My drinking compatriots are the elite nucleus and strength of the Festival, formidable actors all — Bill Hutt, Dougie Campbell, Bruno Gerussi, Max Helpmann, Dougie Rain, Bill Needles, Tony Van Bridge, Robert Christie, Ted Follows and my old pal Bob Goodier. They are giving me a hard time. It's going to be tough being accepted into this fraternity. I'll have to hold my drink with the best of them and still deliver the goods.

All summer long, they made me walk the plank, but they didn't break me or even humble me. What they gave me instead was a fighting spirit I'd never known before. I'm forever grateful for that, and whether they like it or not, I count them my lifelong friends!

The great Guthrie was still in evidence, but a wiry Scot whose academic demeanor concealed many a smouldering fire was our new boss. If Guthrie's genius and panache had given the enterprise a champagne start, Michael Langham was to mature it into a rich, robust, enduring burgundy! It was his vision that brought us our French Connection. He imported the Theatre de Nouveau Monde from Montreal to present their superb Moliere repertoire and to portray the French Court in *Henry* — an inspired stroke of diplomacy. Two vastly contrasting styles and languages now merged into one. There we were, the two solitudes, alive and well on the same stage — something that should occur with regularity in our country but, alas, rarely does. Oh, how sweet when Art triumphs over Politics, even for a whisker of time. The Gauls were among us, their presence a joy. They'd pulled us all together — Jean Gascon, Jean Louis Roulx, Guy Hoffman, Gratien Gelinas, not to mention my beautiful Princesse, Ginette Letondal, and the rest. What a gloriously gregarious group! What ammunition! Together we could have swept the fields at Agincourt, Crecy and Poitier all at once.

Back then, you would not have found any local restaurant listed in *Gourmet* magazine or the *Guide Michelin,* to put it gently. There was good meat and veg at the Queen's Hotel, there was Ellam's all-night diner (I was once barred from Ellam's, what a fall was there!) and, of course, the one and only Chinese eatery, the Golden Bamboo.

On weekends, when everything shut down, we would descend upon the old Walper Inn in Kitchener for roast beef and martinis. (For many years, the Walper was a hangout for Dougie Rain, Kate Reid and myself.) There was good German fare at the Blue Moon in Petersburg (there still is). Angie's Kitchen in St. Agatha was another well-known stop. Otherwise, that was it! As for wines, the Stratford Liquor Board offered nothing much finer than Blue Nun (white) or Sangre de Torro (red), so we generally got swacked on hard stuff and beer chasers.

But when Les Musquatiers arrived — boy, did everything change. They took turns cooking for us in their digs. We would gorge on cassoulets, pizzaladiers, tourtieres and boeuf bourguignons. At last there was the smell of garlic in the streets. Things were looking up. They brought their own wines from *la belle province* and got friendly with the LCBO boys, tactfully advising them on what to stock. Soon we could buy over-the-counter Veuve Cliquot, Pontet Canet or even Chambertin. It wasn't until Robin Phillips's reign as artistic director some years later, however, that Stratford would rival any town in Canada in the art of haute cuisine. Robin's own Church Restaurant, the Belfry (now run by Mark Kraft), James Morris's superb Rundles, Eleanor and Marion's The Old Prune, and others continually try to surpass each other. Cooking schools of exceptional standards attract would-be chefs from all over the country. Even the Festival's Green Room, where once you were lucky to get a warmed-over hot-dog and baked beans, now proudly offers confections of the highest order and some of the town's best grub! But the French had started the ball rolling — Jean Gascon, the chief perpetrator.

Jean, who uniquely ran our country's two major theatres, one French, one English, was *un veritable homme de la Renaissance*. He loved life as passionately as life loved him. I can still hear his booming baritone, with the tinge of whisky-blanc in it, bellowing Moliere, Racine, and jaunty old French *chansons*. A cross between Pantagruel and Francois Premier, he adored playing host to the world. He and his good lady Marilyn's hospitality while in Stratford was extraordinary. I took full advantage of it in my bachelor years — it is not possible to ever repay them. Gascon stayed on as artistic director and a much-loved fixture of the town. He continued to blend our two cultures while ever burning the midnight oil. Then, one day, his gigantic heart (much too big for one human) burst. The only cruel thing he ever did was to leave us all behind for the longest time, lost without him.

The Avon Theatre and City Hall as seen from inside a small café.

A train makes its way through the snow and into St. Mary's station.

Memories of my green years flash by like shadows. I remember the CNR train whistle that regularly shattered the quietest moment in Henry's soliloquy "Upon the King." No matter how hard I tried to speed up or slow down, it persisted in hooting at exactly the same spot night after night. Faking a minor tantrum, I shouted at Tom Patterson to have the train-time changed. I couldn't believe it, he called the CNR and they did just that. Good ol' Tom.

At the back of the Tent was a large hut with enormous glass windows overlooking the river. It was reserved especially for foreign critics. Vultures from the *New York Times*, the *Herald Tribune*, the *London Times*, the *London Observer,* and others could be seen hunched over their desks, furiously scribbling away — in full view of us actors on the slopes below. If we'd had a couple of shotguns and a lot more chutzpah, we could easily have popped them off one by one. But they'd been so good to us, we decided to let them live.

For three weeks of the season, Stratford also boasted a music festival. You could sit in the Golden Bamboo opposite Yehudi Menuhin, Glenn Gould, Dave Brubeck, and Willie "The Lion" Smith, munching away on their egg rolls. Or you might bump into Maureen Forrester, Oscar Peterson, or Benjamin Britten strolling by the river. Julian Bream gave master classes in one of the churches. One night, leaving the stage door, I saw the famous pianist Rudolf Serkin conducting an imaginary orchestra in the parking lot. He spotted me. "I yam cawmpozeeng piano concerto for Hainry Feeft. Fentesticle play! Fentesticle!" And waving his arms to some silent theme, he disappeared up a grassy knoll.

How could I forget the day David Selznick and Jennifer Jones came to a matinee. Selznick wanted me for Dick Diver in his *Tender is the Night,* plus a seven-picture contract. My God, I was going to be famous! But after much agonizing, I dolefully declined the great producer's offer, saying I would prefer to stay where I was, buried in the classics. Was I a schmuck or was I a schmuck?!

Sunbathers enjoy an afternoon of sun and swimming at the Quarry in St. Mary's.

Close by is St. Mary's, a charming little hamlet set on two hills. I often stay there at an inn called the Westover, an elegant country house standing in its own grounds, shaded by huge old maples. It is impeccably run by Julie Docker, Steve McCotter, Reg Jackson, et. al, an attractive group of youngsters who seem to very much know what they're about. The food and wine, in the expert hands of Michael Hoy, are sumptuous. On the outskirts of town is an old quarry. This one is special. In the fifties, on our days off, we would swim in its cool, clear, seemingly bottomless waters. Not many knew about it then — it was ours. We had the place to ourselves. That is until some of the more celebrated of our audience caught on and joined us there. On the raft, sunning themselves, would be Rod Steiger (a regular), Paul Newman and Joanne Woodward (still regulars), Roger Stevens and Robert Whitehead, Maurice Evans, Alan Jay Lerner — even wonderful, crusty old Thornton Wilder. One summer, my dear friend the late, lamented, beauteous Natalie Wood, for whom I've nursed a crush all my life, turned up wearing a swimsuit that almost started a forest fire.

The Queen's Inn at Stratford was established in 1858 by William Johnston.
Today, innkeepers Barb and Larry Ford and their family share a tradition of warm hospitality
as they welcome local guests and those from around the world.

A summer storm approaches Stratford from western Perth County.

The Quarry also proved a perfect hideaway where you could take your girl at dusk and lie in the tall grass, content to smooch the night away. Everything was being taken care of just as nature had planned, when suddenly the soft moanings of other would-be lovers broke the necessary concentration and we realized with sinking hearts that we were by no means alone. Scurrying back into our clothes, we shamefully slunk away, our red faces safely undetected in the gathering darkness.

One sticky Sunday afternoon (the year is fuzzy), we set out for a picnic lunch at the Quarry. It was to celebrate Tony and Judy Guthrie's return from England. The two bird-like Celts loomed over the proceedings, hugely entertaining us. It was a much-married company that year, so there were piles of children and tiny tots. Towards the end of the afternoon, some very thick clouds obliterated the sun and everything turned an ominous black. A strange yellow light formed a border around the darkness. Suddenly, the wind got up and a huge thunderclap told us we should get the hell out of there. We had been so preoccupied with packing our baskets, we hadn't noticed that the very youngest of the children were missing, nowhere to be seen. Frantic mothers ran around in circles, calling out for them. No reply. Panic set in. Then someone shouted, "Look up there! There they are!" Over the brow of the long, steep hill behind us came the imposing figure of Tony Guthrie, one child on his back and two tiny ones on each side, huddled in his arms, which he clasped about them. On either side of them, completing the parade, was a long, straight line of little children, all holding hands. A ray of sun suddenly pierced the clouds, and for a moment they all stood, motionless as in a painting, looking down at us, silhouetted against that fearsome sky. There was utter silence. Only Dougie Campbell managed to whisper, "It's God bringing back his littlest angels." And then everyone moved toward each other and the spell was broken.

Mervyn "Butch" Blake, seen here in front of the Festival Theatre, has acted professionally for over 64 years and has performed in every play that Shakespeare wrote.

The Tent was gone and with it a wonderful sense of living dangerously. Now we had a roof over our heads. We were safe. We were the "only established, permanent crap game" of its kind. The challenge ahead was to sustain the former freshness. Michael Langham managed it masterfully.

With the new building came Mervyn "Butch" Blake, a much-cherished bear of an Englishman, of infinite good nature, richly supported by an infectious giggle. Butch has played every character part in the canon, several times over. (One day you'll get 'em right, Butch!) He's also been captain of the Festival cricket team for as long as I can remember. Butch is a young ninety, and his incredible warmth and magic continue to hold the place together.

Hard on his heels, Paddy Crean followed, straight from *Zenda*, *Gunga Din* and *The Raj*, a handsome, gallant Brit with an astonishing expertise at fencing, and swordsmanship in general, who has coached and doubled some of the screen's greatest stars. The sun never sets on Paddy. He presides over his armoury like a warlord and is forever clicking his heels and saluting everyone, especially the ladies. Errol Flynn, eat your heart out!

All over the county, people threw open their houses to us. We were spoiled rotten. The gorgeous farmland hills outside Sebringville that Gib Jarrott owned became for years our second home. Gib was a well-known doctor, but his life was so taken up with looking after us, his "family," he never seemed to have time for anything else. Gascon affectionately called him *le medecin malgré-lui*. We had the total run of the place, swimming and barbecuing far into the night. Gib and his good wife, Elizabeth, should both be canonized! In Stratford, Dave Rae, Archdeacon Lightbourne, Alf and Dama Bell, among others — some of whom were original board members — never stopped hosting us royally. Dama survived most of them. She is now in her nineties, a distinguished loyal patron, devoted Festival champion, and keeper of the flame.

Gradually the actors, musicians and crew members began to acquire houses, both in town and in the surrounding country, happily settling in with their families the year round, creating for themselves a small but comforting Utopia. It is a rare thing indeed and, in my remembrance, quite unique — art and commerce existing together as they do here, in such relative harmony.

Stratford is well known for its Ontario cottages, many of which have been restored to their original condition.

Two summers ago, I went back to Stratford. Driving up the 401, my mind automatically pressed Rewind and a montage of past images flickered into focus. My daughter Amanda screaming blue murder and splashing in the font while being baptized at St. James Anglican Church one sunny but very noisy afternoon. Jason Robards, having played *Hotspur*, primed to the gills, driving his beloved "Red Ding Dong" to Chicago at 3 A.M. in order to marry wife number two, wearing Tamburlaine's helmet and with an enormous Medusa shield on the front seat beside him. (Only Jason's craggy charm got him through customs.) Max Helpman's Ghost and my Hamlet clinging to each other for dear life lest we fall over the parapet, both of us hopelessly hungover, Max's ghostly green make-up an all-too-clear reminder of how we both felt. An actor who shall remain nameless, Bob Goodier, playing the Chorus in *Romeo and Juliet* one night, a little worse for wear, slurringly rounding out the tragedy with: "There never was a story of more woe / than this of Romi-ette and her Julio...." The touching sight of Doug Campbell's in-laws, Dame Sybil Thorndike and husband Sir Lewis Casson, pillars of the British stage, visiting the Festival, both over ninety but still holding hands — young lovers to the end.

ABOVE: *The main entrance and office mezzanine at the Festival Theatre.*
AT RIGHT: *Autumn on the grounds of St. James Anglican Church.*

Music comes alive in Stratford each summer.
Here, the Stratford Concert Band performs on a Wednesday evening in Queen's Park

And all those memorable evenings of theatre, watching Frances Hyland, John Colicos, Kate Reid, Julie Harris, Siovahnn McKenna, the two Douglases, Rain and Campbell, Frederick Valk, Alec Guiness, Irene Worth, Maggie Smith, Brian Bedford, Tony van Bridge, Paul Scofield, Eileen Herlie, Zoe Caldwell, a young, exciting Martha Henry, and the perennial William Hutt, a longtime Stratford resident whose rich portrayals place him firmly at the top of his profession — and so many others. What an astonishing legacy of work has rocketed this quiet, unsuspecting community.

But stop! I've arrived at the tiny town of Shakespeare.

There was a time when, if you passed through Shakespeare and sneezed, you missed it. Now it is crammed with visitors, by the busloads, as they crowd around Jonny's fascinating antiquities gaping awestruck at his priceless collections of porcelain and china. It's all too tempting. I better hurry on, or he'll nail me!

I dropped by the Festival's offices to say hello to Richard Monette. A fine actor and director, he once, as a youth, played the little slave Eros to my Marc Antony. Richard is now in his fifth season as artistic director, and besides doing excellent work, he has brought the Festival to new financial heights. What a gargantuan leap, from Eros to Caesar!

Stratford Festival Artistic Director Richard Monette
rehearses a scene with actor Diane D'Aquila.

The Avon Theatre.

Next I went down to the Avon Theatre, where my play *Barrymore* was about to make its debut. The Avon has the best crew you could possibly imagine: Jay Klassen, Bruno Hacquebard, John Hoodless, Chris Shaw, Jeremy Lach, Gord Balmain, Mark Fisher, Dan Hoodless, Scott Mathews, Martin Penner and Harry Van Keuren — pros and stalwarts all — the very backbone of the place. At the day's end, we all repair to Susan Dunfield's Down the Street, a warm, friendly *boîte* full of wise saws and modern instances where gossip is king.

Oh, yes, the town has changed, all right, no doubt about it. It may have lost a little of its heart along the way, but, by god, 'tis a far, far better place than I once knew. It thrives, it flourishes. The shops are shinier, tearooms are aplenty, art is for sale on the riverbanks, not a corner of it is unused. Carnival is in the air and, yes, you can stay too long at the fair. Louis Appelbaum's old fanfares are more elaborate, there is a sense of general prosperity, and everything has a little more flair. Just as the great Highland chieftans were piped in to dinner, so the swans are no less ceremoniously piped to the water's edge each spring.

On the last Sunday in March,
the swans are ceremoniously piped from their winter home to the Avon River.

Tom Patterson Island illuminated for the holiday season.

But summer's lease has all too short a date and now they must waddle back behind the Arena to join their feathered friends under the watchful eye of the local St. Francis, Robert Miller. For the last tourist has taken his leave, the trees are bare, and the falling snow begins to silence all about it. Only the Christmas lights on Tom Patterson's Island glitter away to remind us of the man and his dream. The good people of Perth County "like sacrifices by their watchful fires sit patiently" and wait for the next season to burst upon them like arrows on the Feast of Crispian. And Stratford, under a carpet of white, cannot wait to recapture the old rhythm it once knew, and with a great sigh of relief it goes to sleep, for the time being at least, quite deservedly pleased with itself and more than a little blessed.

Christopher Plummer

*Early morning mist
near Prospect Hill.*

A monument stands along Highway 8
to commemorate the early settlers of Perth County.

Sunflowers near Sebringville.

Quiet time at Wildwood Lake.

ABOVE: *One of Stratford's several beautiful parks, the Shakespearean Gardens,*
located along the Avon River west of the Huron Street bridge.

AT RIGHT: *Autumn in Queen's Park.*

Fountains and flowers provide a peaceful setting for Canadian Fabricated Products on Erie Street in Stratford.

Confederation Park, a civic centennial project, was built as a Japanese-style garden.

ABOVE: *An English-style Tudor manor on William Street*
looks out onto the Avon River and the Festival Theatre.

AT LEFT: *66 Queen, one of Stratford's many quaint bed-and-breakfasts.*

ABOVE: *Stratford City Hall, built in 1898, decorated for the holidays.*

AT LEFT: *Reflections and souvenirs in a downtown store window.*

The Stratford Farmers' Market, located at the fairgrounds, is a popular attraction for tourists and locals alike, and opens its doors every Saturday morning year-round.

Despite the fact that Stratford boasts some of the finest restaurants in the country, everyone still enjoys the street vendor's friendly smile and his barbecued cuisine.

A Christmas window along Ontario Street.

Down the Street bar and café is a popular spot for theatregoers, actors, stagehands and staff.

Wade's Flowers, established in 1953, is a family-run gift and flower shop.

Bentley's Inn and Bar is a favourite meeting place for locals in the winter, and for tourists when the Theatre opens.

OPPOSITE
Quaint shops along York Street.

*A summer sidewalk sale
in downtown Stratford.*

*Some of the best home-cooking in town,
at the York Street Kitchen.*

One of Stratford's original businesses, Watson's Chelsea Bazaar,
is an import and retail business that was founded by the Bradshaw family in 1834.

The newly renovated Festival Theatre,
the beneficiary of Act III,
a $15-million renovation campaign.

The "Avon crew" poses on the stage with Stratford Festival founder Tom Patterson.

Paddy Crean, former fight-scene director for the theatre, strikes a pose in the armoury located in the Festival Theatre.

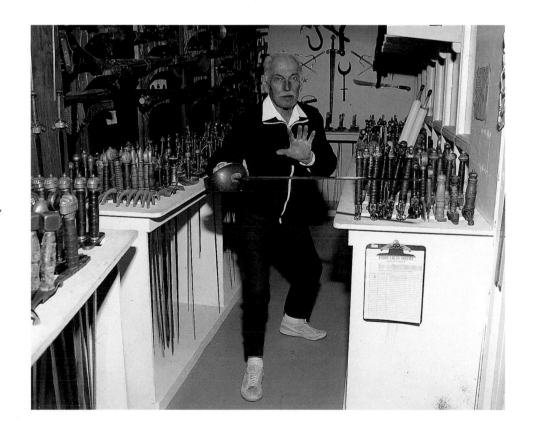

OPPOSITE:
The stage door to the Tom Patterson Theatre.

Working on costumes for an upcoming performance.

ABOVE AND AT LEFT: *Props and costumes at the costume warehouse.*

Building new props at the Festival Theatre "prop shop."

Stratford Festival music director Bert Carrière conducts the orchestra from the loft above the Festival Theatre stage.

Interior featuring the stage at the Festival Theatre.

*Order of Canada recipient Dama Bell has been an active
supporter of the Stratford Festival since its early years.
She also maintains an extensive collection of
costume design sketches dating back to 1953.*

*Monument to commemorate
the Act III renovation project.*

ABOVE: *The bridge to Tom Patterson Island.*

AT LEFT: *The Festival Theatre.*

OVERLEAF: *A frozen Avon River and the Theatre wait patiently for next season.*

ABOVE: *The Perth County Court House.*

PREVIOUS PAGE: *The illuminated Huron Street bridge over the Avon River at dusk.*

The interior of Knox Presbyterian Church, consecrated in 1873.

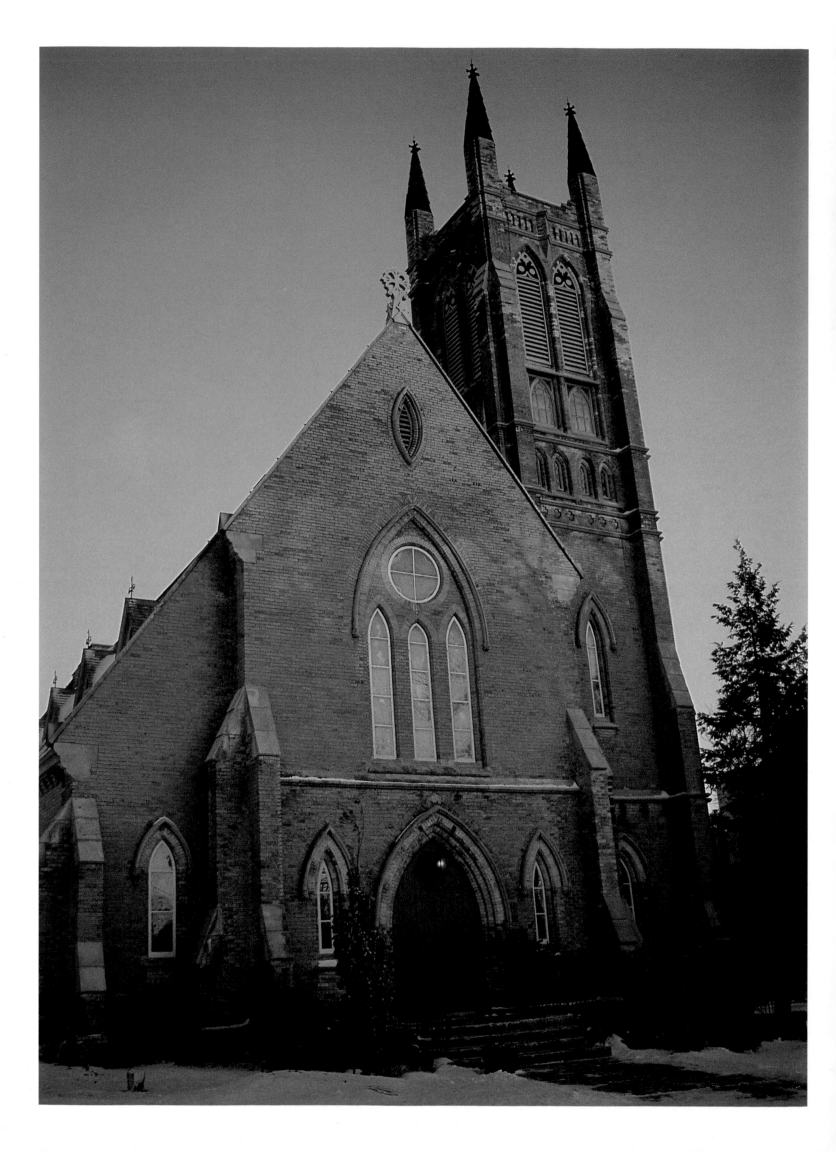

The Bells of St. James and the bell ringer's "keyboard."

AT LEFT:

St. James Anglican Church, founded in 1840, is a city landmark and noted for its Bells of St. James. The present church was built in 1870, and the bells were installed in 1909.

ABOVE: *Hidden from most passers-by is a relief panel of Shakespeare found between the Tudor framing of this downtown building.*

AT RIGHT: *One of Stratford's finest, the Church Restaurant and Belfry.*

ABOVE: *The renowned Stratford Chefs School is a private non-profit institution
co-founded by James Morris, from Rundles Restaurant, and Eleanor Kane, from the Old Prune.*

AT LEFT: *A quiet table amid original art at the Old Prune Restaurant.*

Festival tours depart from Memorial Gardens
aboard this authentic English double-decker bus.

Lawn bowling on the greens at the Stratford Lawn Bowling Club.

One of summer's many celebrations, Art in the Park.

The Kirkin' o' the Tartan,
an event held each August at Knox Presbyterian Church.

The Lion's Pool.

The Stratford Fall Fair.

Canada Day celebrations
at the Stratford Education and Recreation Centre.

A tour trolley makes its way around the Avon River.

The Stratford Dragon Boat Races, held each September, are run and sponsored by the Stratford Rotary Club.

OVERLEAF: *Dragon boats race toward the finish line.*

Stratford's resident "St. Francis"
and honourary keeper of the swans, Robert Miller.

Early spring, and the swans arrive
to a partially ice-covered Avon River.

*Winter along the Avon River
below the Dam.*

Early morning along the Avon.

Autumn harvest along Highway 7 near Wildwood Lake.

Local Amish residents
return from Sunday church services near Milverton.

At a market in Millbank, Amish farmers
gather around a wagon filled with local produce.

Amish worshippers at Sunday church services near Millbank.

ABOVE: *A collection from the past on Highway 7 near St. Paul's.*

AT RIGHT: *The old post office in Sebringville.*

ABOVE: *Stepping back in time at an old mill in Sebringville.*

AT LEFT: *One of the many antique shops in Shakespeare.*

Outside Jonny's Antiques in Shakespeare.

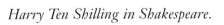

Harry Ten Shilling in Shakespeare.

*An early winter morning
in St. Mary's.*

"Little Falls" on the Thames River in St. Mary's.

ABOVE AND OVERLEAF: *The Westover Inn in St. Mary's was built in 1867 by the Hutton brothers as their family home and opened as a country inn in 1987. The inn features 22 guest rooms and exceptional dining.*

*And Stratford, under a carpet of white,
cannot wait to recapture the old rhythm
it once knew, and with a great sigh
of relief it goes to sleep, for the time being
at least, quite deservedly pleased with itself
and more than a little blessed.*

CHRISTOPHER PLUMMER

ACKNOWLEDGMENTS

I moved from Stratford when I was ten years old. Never did I imagine that someday I would return with a camera to capture the spirit of this wonderful place that I still call home. I hope that these photographs bring back as many memories for you as taking them did for me.

It was a great honour to have Christopher Plummer agree to write the foreword for this book. Mr. Plummer's many fond memories of this city and the surrounding area are evidenced in his written reflections. A very special thank-you goes to Betty Michalyshyn of SPI–Special Projects International Inc., whose support, moral and material, has seen this book to its fruition.

So many people contributed to this production. Thanks to Richard Monette, Karen Harmer, Anita Gaffney, Elke Bidner, and the entire production and technical staff at the Stratford Festival. Thanks also to Barb and Larry Ford and the staff from the Queen's Inn; Mark Kraft from the Church Restaurant; Peter and Heather Pryde; Alex Mayer; Joan Parsons; Barb Quarry and Cathy Rehberg from Tourism Stratford; David Lester; and Kodak Canada.

During the time spent photographing this book I met so many people and learned much about this community and its theatre. It was an incredible experience to have the opportunity to meet and to hear stories of the early theatre from Tom Patterson, Mervyn "Butch" Blake and Dama Bell, and to spend time talking to local residents who shared stories of the early days of "Stratford the railway town."

I dedicate this book to my parents, Glen and Barbara Bain, who were such a part of this community until we moved away in 1965. They have shared many of their own memories with me, and I am grateful for their support during this project. I am saddened that my father did not live to see this book published. However, he did see much of the work-in-progress and was always delighted to see my latest roll of slides when I returned from a shoot.

To my children, Daniel and Caroline, who didn't see much of Dad during this time, thanks for your love and understanding. I hope that these photographs remind you of time that we spend together feeding the swans in summer.

Finally, to all the people of Stratford, and to Joan, my hometown friend, thank you for all that you did to make this city the special place that it is. I also dedicate this book to you. May Stratford always be home to you, as it will always be home to me.

Richard Bain